Don't You Dare! A story about making safe choices

Written and Illustrated by Tenille Dowe

Copyright © 2025 Tenille Dowe

All rights reserved. No part of this book may be reproduced in any manner whatsoever without prior written permission of the publisher.

First Printing, 2025

Published by Creative Heart Connection
www.creativeheartconnection.com

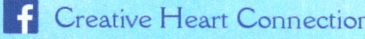
Creative Heart Connection

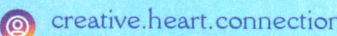
creative.heart.connection

ISBN 978-1-7636536-7-2

Making friends can be tough, sometimes the road feels rough.

Just be kind and have a go,
you never know who you might get to know.

If someone dares you to do something wrong,
be brave and say no!

That shows you're strong.

Her best friend was her cat,
so small and so sweet.
With tiny soft paws and quick little feet.
They'd cuddle each night, never far apart.

She loved her fluffball
with all of her heart.

Together they played,
a purr-fect pair from the start.

Her friends dared her to bring her cat to school.
They said it'd be funny and make her look cool,
she shook her head.
She knew that's not the rule.......

Sometimes to keep friends happy,
we might do something funny.

A friend might say, "I dare you."
It could cost you more than money.

Before you jump in
and follow the crowd,
stop and think........

STOP, Don't You Dare!

Cats belong at home, snuggling on the lounge.
Not in your backpack
where they'd wriggle and scrounge.

They like a warm spot and a soft bed,
with pats on their back and a scratch on their head.
School's not the place for a meow or a purr.
So leave your cat home where it's happy for sure.

Cats belong in the garden chasing blue butterflies,
leaping through leaves under bright sunny skies.
Not hiding in backpacks or sneaking to school.
They're happiest at home.
That is the golden rule.

Cats don't belong on a school bus ride,
with bumps and noise and nowhere to hide.
They're happier at home, safe inside.

Cats don't belong in the principal's office.
He's shy and scared, not ready for this.
He should be at home, not causing a fuss.

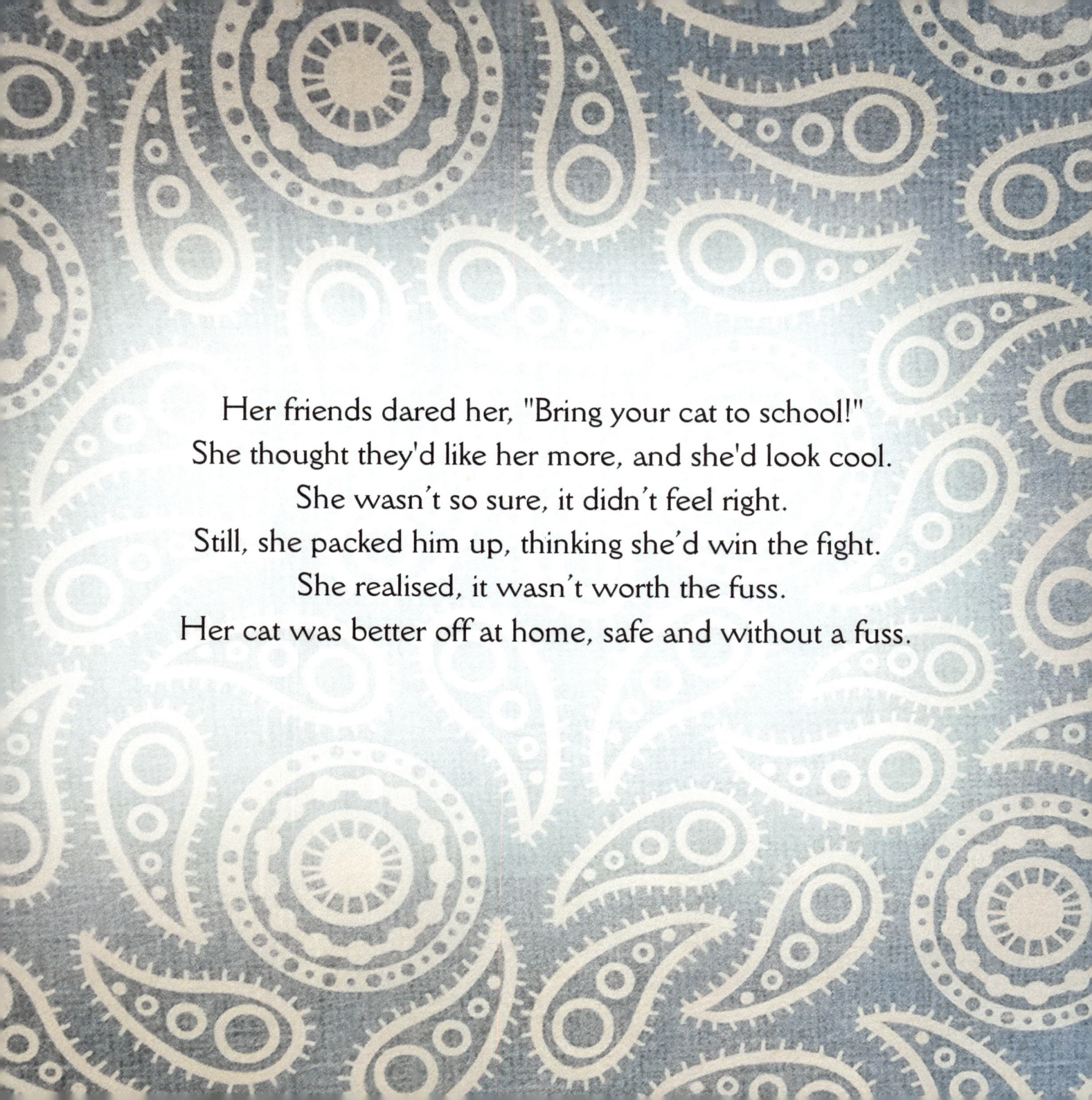

Her friends dared her, "Bring your cat to school!"
She thought they'd like her more, and she'd look cool.
She wasn't so sure, it didn't feel right.
Still, she packed him up, thinking she'd win the fight.
She realised, it wasn't worth the fuss.
Her cat was better off at home, safe and without a fuss.

The cat made himself comfy in the principal's office.
Rolling on the desk,
feeling relieved and more at ease.

If you're unsure about a dare from a friend,
ask a trusted adult.
It's the best way for this to end.
They'll help you decide what's safe and wise,
so you don't get caught by a bad surprise.

Sometimes, friends might dare you
to do something they think could be funny.
It could go wrong, not sweet like honey.
You might feel pressure to join the crowd, trust yourself.
You're brave and proud.

Dares are not always safe.

She was asked to cut her own hair on a dare.
They laughed and said, "Go on, if you dare!"
She knew it wasn't right, it just felt wrong.
The pressure from her friends was loud and strong.

There he was, fast asleep,
tucked in her backpack.
Curled up tight, not a sound, or a peep.

She was bored at home,
with nothing much to do.
So she chatted with friends, online.
There were quite a few.
They laughed and reminded her of the dare from before,
to cut her own hair, though she wasn't quite sure.

She said, "Maybe not now"......
Her friends were relentless, she couldn't ignore.

She spotted the scissors on the bathroom bench.

Her heart gave a thump, her hands felt a clench.

She thought of the dare and stood there in doubt.......

Should she snip her hair, or just back out?

Then the bathroom door creaked open a bit.

Her cat closed his eyes as if he didn't want to stay......

He was wishing this moment would just go away.

Mum walked in and gave a sigh........

"You cut your hair for a dare?"
"Oh love, but why?"

She frowned and said,

"That choice wasn't safe to try."

Mum spoke to her in a gentle but firm tone.

"When friends dare you, you're not on your own. Think it through before you decide, the safest choice is always your best guide."

Tears welled up in her eyes, as Mum reminded her again to be wise and remember........

Remember....
STOP,
Don't You Dare!

"There's no need to apologise,"
Mum said with care.

"They're not real friends if
they're giving that dare.
True friends keep you safe
and are always fair."

The following morning, up early, bright and keen.
She packed her school bag, neat and clean.
Books stacked in tight, ready for the day.
Learning and laughter were on the way.

Waiting for the bus with a funky new hair style,
she remembered the rule...
Stop, don't you dare! Dares are not cool.
Even if friends think it's just a joke,
one silly move and the fun could go up in smoke.

Remember, cats belong in the garden, having fun, chasing bright butterflies and snoozing in the sun. Not at school, even if your friends dare you just for fun.

www.ingramcontent.com/pod-product-compliance
Lightning Source LLC
Chambersburg PA
CBHW041103070526
44583CB00002B/39